every girl tells a story

They

all want

to get in

with the "in"

crowd.

—Julie, 15

There are

a lot of children

who aren't

as lucky as I.

—Hilary, 14

My parents

showed

me it's

okay to be

myself.

—Lindsey, 18

I've really

worked hard

and it's

paid off.

—Kendra, 15

Girl Scouts®

every girl tells a story

a celebration of girls speaking their minds by carolyn jones

in collaboration with **Girl Scouts of the USA** foreword by First Lady Laura Bush

The choices you

make today

completely affect you

two years from now,

twenty-two years

from now.

—Natalie, 16

If your

heart's in it,

you'll keep

going.

—Therese, 14

People don't

need to fight

over how

they pray . . .

just as long as

they pray.

—Angel, 13

I'd like

to open a

clinic for women

and children

in Iran. That has

always been

my dream.

—Leila, 17

simon & schuster

new york

london

toronto

sydney

singapore

acknowledgments

From Girls Scouts of the USA

Carolyn Jones, photographer, for her art and insight
All the girls who participated in the project, for their generosity and vision
Individuals from Girl Scouts of the USA:
Connie L. Matsui, National President
Marty Evans, National Executive Director
Joyce Richards, National Director, Marketing and Development
Laurie Westley, National Director, Government Relations
Liz Sheppard, Senior Director, Marketing and Communications
Suzanna Penn, Director, Publishing
Diana Pike, Director, Development—Council Funding
Jennifer Yarbrough, Development Consultant, Grants (Photoshoot Coordinator)
Mikki Morrissette, Assistant Photoshoot Coordinator
Sue Turin, Manager, Training and Conference Operations
Peter Stafford, Director, Operations, Edith Macy Conference Center (photoshoot site)
The entire staff at Edith Macy Conference Center

From Carolyn Jones

Many people came together to make this book happen, and
I express my gratitude to all of them:
Everyone at Girl Scouts of the USA who touched this project
Brenda Bowen, my editor
Lee Wade, who designed this book, for her creative guidance
Dennis Lee, photographer's assistant, who was beside me for every interview
Carolina Santos, teacher, High School for Leadership and
  Public Service, New York City
Ada Dolch, Principal, High School for Leadership and
  Public Service, New York City
Ellen Marino, for finding the girls who are not Girl Scouts
Alison Sandler, for helping me organize the project
Betsy Davis, for the hand-painted backdrop
Kathy Grove, for stunning photographic prints
Lou Orza from the Briarcliffe Bike Shop, for lending a bike without question
Jodi Buren, Jodie Healey, Monica Windsor, and Barbara von Schreiber,
  my dear friends, for their help and encouragement
Jacques, my husband, who read every word, looked at every image, and listened

SIMON & SCHUSTER BOOKS FOR YOUNG READERS
An imprint of Simon & Schuster Children's Publishing Division
1230 Avenue of the Americas
New York, New York 10020

SIMON & SCHUSTER BOOKS FOR YOUNG READERS is a trademark of Simon & Schuster.
Book design by Lee Wade and Anne Scatto
The text of this book is set in Caslon 540.
Printed in the United States of America
2 4 6 8 10 9 7 5 3 1

Library of Congress Cataloging-in-Publication Data
Jones, Carolyn (Carolyn Elizabeth)
Every girl tells a story: a celebration of girls speaking their minds / by Carolyn Jones in collaboration with Girl Scouts of the USA.
p. cm.
Summary: Presents the attitudes and achievements of a diverse group of girls between the ages of
thirteen and eighteen living across the United States through portraits and their own words.
ISBN 0-689-84872-2
1. Teenage girls—United States—Case studies. 2. Girls—United States—Case studies.
[1. Teenage girls. 2. Self-actualization.] I. Girl Scouts of the United States of America
HQ798.J629 2002
305.235—dc21
2001055117

FIRST EDITION

To every girl, everywhere—
May your visions be fulfilled. . . .
May your voices be heard. . . .

to young readers

After meeting girls from all over the country, I can safely tell you one thing for sure. Even the prettiest, smartest, most impressive girl you know has questions, fears, concerns, and issues. So take a deep breath. The girls you'll meet in this book are not so very different from you.

To make *Every Girl Tells a Story,* we searched the country for young women between the ages of thirteen and eighteen. All of them felt they had something to say, a story to tell. I asked every young woman to be photographed in clothing that she picked out herself, so she could be seen as she wanted to be seen. Many brought something or wore something that represents their passions and what they most love in life. This is their book, these are their pictures, their words, their thoughts.

Every single girl here has done something achievable. Some of the girls have overcome personal tragedies, perhaps lost a parent, or triumphed in their own encounters with illness. Their perspectives are unique because they had to experience something at a young age that most of us don't encounter until we are older.

Some girls learned lessons that others never learn in a lifetime. Some just took a small opportunity and made it blossom.

A lot of the girls in this book joined organizations because their school required community service hours. Not every girl was born with an innate desire to help others. These young women found their passions in a lot of those organizations. When five hours were required, very often two hundred hours were done. Not out of necessity, but out of passion.

To the girls in this book and girls everywhere I'd say that there are issues in the world. We know that. Those of us ahead of you didn't do it all right; we just did the best we knew how to do. You will all

DENNIS LEE

inherit those issues and problems and we want to know what you are thinking. As we get older, the world seems so vast and the problems so great that the solutions often become bigger and harder to accomplish. Your perspective reminds us that we are all individual people on this planet together and simple kindnesses—helping just one person—can make a huge difference. Staying connected is key. Communicating is everything. No one is ever really alone.

We want to know what you have to say. Talk to us. We're listening. Sometimes we forget to ask, but your vision, your opinions, your solutions are the future.

It was my honor to meet, photograph, and interview the girls in this book. They are our future, and you know what? I think we are in very good hands.

Carolyn Jones
NEW YORK CITY, 2001

foreword

As a former public school teacher, Girl Scout, and the mother of twin daughters, I know every girl has a unique perspective on the world around her, and a unique way of expressing that perspective. In *Every Girl Tells a Story*, we meet eighty-five young women who reflect on the lessons they've learned, the choices they've made, and the hopes they hold for the future.

Kendra, one of six African-American students chosen to attend a high school for gifted students, is bringing her school a new awareness of diversity.

Therese has discovered that if you believe in yourself, you can accomplish any goal; and Lindsey, helped by her parents' unconditional love, realized it's okay to be who you are.

Thirteen-year-old Angel's wise words are especially timely: "People don't need to fight over how they pray."

Two Girl Scouts celebrate the rewards of volunteering. They helped convert an old building in Puerto Rico into a transitional home for abandoned children with no place to go once they grow too old to remain in orphanages.

Although not all of the girls in this book are Girl Scouts, all of their stories echo Girl Scout values: Be honest and fair. Be courageous and strong. Take responsibility. Respect others. And do your best to make the world a better place.

Through perseverance and faith in themselves, these girls are on their way to becoming strong women who will help lead our nation in the future.

My hope for every girl, everywhere, is that she, too, will find her voice and achieve her dreams.

Laura Bush

Mrs. Laura Bush
NATIONAL HONORARY PRESIDENT
GIRL SCOUTS OF THE USA

"I'd like to open a clinic for women

Most people from my state have German ancestors on both sides. And my mom's side is German, but my dad . . . he's from Iran. So that's very different. He's from Sabzevar, a very isolated little town that's two hours from the big religious city, Mashhad. And so my dad, when he came to America . . . it was a big culture shock.

I wouldn't really want to live in Iran because I have more personal freedoms here. If a girl's raped in a Middle Eastern country, sometimes she's killed. It just depends on the country and the family.

get the same things that I want. Because I could go to any college I want, but if girls in Iran want to go to a college, they have to be extremely brilliant. I mean *extremely*. They have to learn Arabic, Persian, English, and everything you can think of. It just amazes me.

At some point, either right after I become a doctor, or maybe even twenty years later, I'd like to go back to Iran. And especially I'd like to open a clinic for women and children in Sabzevar. When I went there, I knew that is what I wanted to do. That has always been my dream.

and children in Iran. That has always been my dream."—Leila, 17

In Sabzevar, all my aunts and my cousins wear this sheet sort of thing called a chador. Only your face is showing and your hands. And your feet have to be covered. No shorts. No short-sleeved shirts. My dad's mom, my grandmother, is extremely conservative and extremely religious. She's constantly praying and reading the Koran. The first time we went to Iran, it was right before a religious holiday and she refused to hear any happy music. It's part of what she does. She's very, very, very devoted and it's just extremely strange for me. One of my Iranian cousins, she's a year older than me. She has been studying basically her whole life to get into college, and luckily she did. But I see how she has to struggle so much more than me to

My mom and I started talking one day and I asked her, "Mom, is there a possibility that I have ADD, or ADHD?"

I was talking about attention deficit disorders. Because I realized it was really hard in high school for me to get my homework done after school; it tired me out during the day. It was just too much all at once and it would just get to me.

I also started having massive emotional breakdowns, where I'd sit in the corner of my room, balled up in a little ball, crying my eyes out, rocking back and forth, saying I wanted to be five. The thing that really scared me was not knowing what it was.

Once I found out it was ADHD, and that I could get some help for it, I was okay.

My mom and I have had our problems . . . we've had our fights. We've gone through me moving out. We've gone through me moving back in. She's read my diary. But we've gotten over it. And my mom has come to realize that I'm not the perfect little girl that I was, or that my parents pictured I'd be, when I was five. I'm my own person, and I'm going my own way.

The best thing my parents have done for me is to show me it's okay to be myself, that they're going to love me anyway. I screw up, and they're still going to love me. Unconditional love. That's it.

"The best thing my parents have done for me is to show me that it's okay to be myself."
—Lindsey, 18

I play softball, basketball, volleyball, cross-country, and track. I started tee ball when I was five years old, and I've been playing softball ever since. Never skipped a season. It teaches me teamwork and how to work with others. And it gives me something to look forward to. So it's always cool—I have something to do in the afternoon.

I know I definitely want to play for the USA Softball Women's National Team in the Olympics. That's something I want to do. I want to be the catcher for the U.S. Olympic team. I hate when people say sports are just for guys. I know a lot of people who are always saying things like, "Oh, she's a tomboy." I just like playing sports.

I was not good when I started and it just takes a lot of practice. You get better as the years go on. And a lot of practice helps.

Just go for it. Keep trying. You'll get better. If your heart's in it, you'll keep going. Girls can do anything. Girls rule.

My mother used to do drugs a lot, so they took me and my sisters away. I never lived with my mother. I lived in foster care until I was seven. I wasn't really comfortable there. I moved to the home of the lady I live with now when I was eight years old. I got over a lot of stuff recently because I started counseling. I was mad about everything. I felt: Everybody gets to be with her mother except for me. I felt abandoned, like I'm nobody. I saw my mother recently and I said, "Did you call me on Monday?" And she said, "What was Monday?" I said, "The Monday we just had." And then she said, "Your birthday?" When I said yes, she told me, Oh, I forgot. I felt so stupid. There was nothing I could do about it. I didn't get it: How could you forget the day you gave birth?

The woman I live with now has a lot of foster kids because she likes foster kids. She's real nice. She takes us all out to eat. We go shopping. She does a lot of things with us. You could tell she doesn't keep us for the money, because one foster kid doesn't pay you enough for you to go out and spend all that money on clothes . . . and it's not cheap clothes. She always keeps us dressed nice and well fed. She adopted me at eleven.

I had no mother role model, so I didn't know how to treat her. She was always there, though. I used to test people to see if they would still be with me. I used to push people away a lot because I would rather do it to them before they did it to me, because that's the way I thought. She just never gave up on me. So I started noticing. If she didn't care for me, why would she keep me this long? And why would she do all the things she does for me? So I started appreciating everything she did.

For Mother's Day I decided to design my own card. It's like a book, and I drew flowers and wrote a poem dedicated to her. A mom is not someone who just gives birth, but someone who fills her children's needs and pushes them to be successful. There are no words for everything she's done for me. No matter what, she's there.

"The thing I'd like to change in the world is foster care."
—Shaday, 14

I never wanted to be like my birth mother. I want to have a point. Why would I want to be on a corner, with AIDS, fifty-something, begging people for money? I want to be able to stand for myself. So I push for myself. Whatever I don't have, whatever I didn't get when I was younger, I want to get it for myself. I like to be independent, because that's what's really going to help me get through.

The thing I'd like to change in the world is foster care. I feel that if you're going to have a kid, you should think about it first, because it may not affect you as much as it affects the kid. If your mother is alive but you can't be with her, it feels like there's something that belongs to you but you can't have it. And I think if you're going to have a kid, you should be responsible enough to take care of it because you were the one who made the decision to have the kid, you and your partner. And that's your responsibility.

I've always had a drive to work with people with disabilities. I worked at a camp for girls with disabilities, with about sixty to ninety girls. There are thirty-six counselors, called "campettes." We went through training, and learned how to lift somebody out of the wheelchair and onto a shower chair or how to dress the girls. We practiced on our peers, brushing their teeth and washing their faces.

At the camp there were some girls who could do almost everything without help, and there were some who didn't have enough mobility to push themselves, even in an electric wheelchair.

The campers were anywhere from eight to twenty-five years old. If they needed it, we would help them get dressed, brush their teeth, feed them. I've talked to a lot of people about this and they say, "Isn't it so sad that you see all these people with disabilities? Isn't it so sad that they can't do all that stuff for themselves and you had to be there to brush their teeth and to feed them?"

But . . . it was really the most uplifting experience of my entire life because you look at these girls and the minute they come into the camp their faces light up. You talk to their parents on the first day and the parents tell you that their daughter says that this is the only place that she can go and be normal.

My job that summer was to help these kids have the best summer of their entire lives. We didn't get a lot of personal time. Everything was for the girls: No matter what we did, no matter where we went, the girls came first. It was as if we were their eyesight, we were their ears, we were whatever they needed us to be. Being able to put myself completely aside and fulfill that role—to be there to help these girls—was absolutely amazing.

It strengthened my drive to help people with disabilities. It strengthened my resolve and narrowed down my career choices. I realized that this was what I wanted to be doing for the rest of my life, to get this feeling of just absolutely helping somebody. You know what I mean?

"It was really the most uplifting experience of my entire life."—Krystel, 17

My family is involved in the military: My father used to be in the air force, and my mother and father both are involved in civil air patrol. The civil air patrol is the United States Air Force Auxiliary. They basically have a three-fold program: cadet programs, aerospace education, and emergency services.

I remember when I was young my father was a pilot, and he flew on missions to look for downed people that had crashed in planes or needed emergency aid. I was there once when someone needed to be rescued and it interested me so much that I decided I wanted to do it too.

Civil air patrol is completely voluntary. Basically we are all trained on our own personal time. Training takes up a lot of personal time; air patrol takes up tons of time. But the training I got could help save somebody's life.

In general, I think the best way to help anyone when they're in any trouble or when they need anything is to support them as much as you can. You can

"The training I got could help save somebody's life."—Claire, 16

help them; you can do whatever. The best thing that I know of is just to be there for the person. If they need to talk, listen to them. Let them lean on you; let them depend on you. That's the best thing you can do. Ever since I was younger I've seen other people needing help. I have friends that are in the emergency services field. It has always interested me to find a way to make a difference and help people.

My interest in being in the military came from the discipline and the motivation that all the people in the military share. They're all very motivated and they want to work together for a common goal. I think Girl Scouts helped me become disciplined. It has helped me a lot, especially with teamwork. Now I think I want to be in the medical field, maybe as an emergency medical technician or a medical service technician in the military. My experience in the air patrol has shown me that when I'm in my uniform, I respect my uniform, I respect what it stands for, and I feel extremely comfortable doing that.

"Being admitted to that school did change my life."—Kendra, 15

When I was in fifth grade, I was chosen to be in the Scholar Middle School for the Gifted and Talented. Being admitted to that school did change my life. If I had gone to the public junior high, I would have been teased all the time for being smart. The Scholar School makes you realize that you can do something, that you can do better things with your life.

Now I'm in a rich suburban high school in a program called the PSP School. It's kind of like a boarding school, but not exactly. I live with a family in a house with six other girls from the PSP. It's pretty much like living in a normal house except you have five other sisters and a mom and dad who aren't exactly your mom and dad, and a little brother who's not exactly your brother.

I live in this really rich town. There's nothing but rich people living there. And then it's not diverse at all. Not at all. I can count on my hand the number of black people in that town. You have Asians, and then the rest are just white. But you have to get used to it after a while. The only black people that you see are the people that you live with.

I feel like I always have to do my best in everything, since otherwise I'd hear about it, even from other kids. Like, "Oh, I thought she was supposed to be smart. What happened? What happened?" I feel I always will do my best in everything because my dad's always telling me, Whatever you do, do it to your best ability. I think that because of being labeled "gifted and talented," I have to work harder so I can live up to that title.

I want to do a Black History assembly in school next year. It kind of made me angry that this year no one mentioned that it was Black History Month, and there are six black kids in the school. We're not doing anything to recognize it. It's celebrated all over and this one little town is shut off from it as if it doesn't exist. I want to make an assembly, let everyone know that it is Black History Month. And if you don't want to celebrate then you don't have to. But I just want you to be aware of it.

I've really worked hard and it's paid off. So now I know that I'm going to get a good education and I'll hopefully go to a good college and this way I'll be successful and I'll have that life that—well, I don't know if everyone dreams of it, but hopefully I'll have that life that a lot of people dream of.

In eighth grade I was diagnosed with epilepsy. Up until that time I was on high honor roll. I never really had to study; learning just came naturally. I would hear information in class and remember it. But when they put me on all these different medications for epilepsy, I didn't grasp information like I used to, so my grades went down. I started ninth grade taking three honors classes and one college prep class, which was well above what everybody else was doing, but because things didn't come to me the way they used to, I wasn't able to hold on to all of my classes. It was really hard because my classes and my grades—that was me. I thought, Okay, I'm smart, and I have all this potential; but when I couldn't do the work I used to do, it really brought me down. I started beating myself up a lot.

My mom just kept telling me, if you try hard, you can do this. So I kept trying, I kept trying, I kept trying. And I have been able to bring my grades back up. Just this past August they took me off my medicine and I'm fine now. This year I started the year with two advanced placement classes and one honors class. So I'm back where I would have been. I'm extremely proud of myself. Now I know that as long as I try and stay positive I can overcome anything. That's what I learned from my mother.

"I kept trying."
—Leslie, 17

"I can't live without music."
—Aja, 16

My name is Aja and I got my name from a song that my mom loved: Steely Dan's "Aja," of course. I have that record hanging up on my wall. I love that record. One thing about myself is that I love to sing. I can't live without music.

I think if I had to make a choice today of what my career in life will be, it would probably be music in the performing arts. My first toy was a microphone. I still have it in my dresser drawer. I just can't live without music. It's in my soul and I just . . . I have to carry it everywhere with me.

I sing at school for girls' basketball games, and I sing in the choir. I also sing the National Anthem at different places around the state. I've sung for different women's teams of Minnesota—hockey, and basketball, and gymnastics, things like that. And I also sing for the Minnesota Twins.

At a game, when I am going to sing the National Anthem, I have to go to some secluded place. I have to get my thoughts together and think of what I'm singing. It has to be in my heart and in my mind. I'm singing our National Anthem, and it's representing the whole entire United States. So I have to think about this beforehand, and then I go out there and I do my best to sing it right.

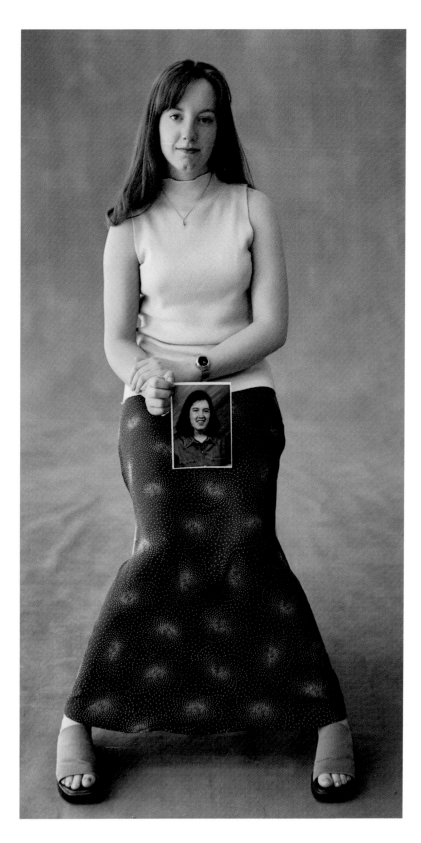

Stephanie is my fraternal twin sister. I'm twin A and the firstborn, and Stephanie is twin B. We were born three months premature. We have completely different personalities. She likes meat and I don't like meat; I love bread. She has brown hair and I have lighter hair. I have blue eyes and she has brown eyes. She's a lot shorter than me. So, aside from genetics, we're pretty different.

"A lot of people use the phrase,

Usually, if twins have problems, it's twin B who has the most trouble. Stephanie is handicapped in a few ways. She's developmentally delayed. She goes to a different school where they spend a lot of one-on-one time with her. You can tell when you talk to her. She's a good conversationalist, but you can tell. It's hard to explain. Physically, her left hand and her left side don't really work well. Her eyes used to be "lazy"—crossed together. She had surgery when she was real young to have that fixed. But sometimes if she concentrates, her eyes still go together.

She was fine when she was born, but not long afterward she had a grade-four brain bleed. It's like a stroke when you're a baby. It makes me sad because I think, What if it was me? A lot of people don't understand. They just haven't ever been around a person who's disabled. A lot of people feel sorry for someone with disabilities. That's really not how you should feel. If you're going to talk to a person who's developmentally delayed, just treat them like a normal person. Don't talk down to them, that kind of thing. Don't be conde-

because it's just so offensive. It just shows a kind of ignorance.

Sometimes Stephanie, she gets real exuberant when she meets new people. She might come out and start telling them she loves music and she has so many CDs and she knows the number and the name of every album. And I'll think, you know, Stephanie, they don't need to know that, so just don't tell them about it. But then I see it's what

'Oh, that's so retarded.' That just completely sets me off."—Amy, 14

scending. If someone talks to Stephanie condescendingly, she knows it. She's got intuition that says, I'm smarter than that.

A lot of people use the phrase, "Oh, that's so retarded." That just completely sets me off. I know they say that because they don't understand. They think people like that are stupid. Completely not the case.

I'll explain to people that my sister is disabled and they'll say, "Oh, she's retarded." And I say, "Well, if you want to think of it like that, I guess you can, but I don't really like to use that term." If you ever meet someone who is disabled, you'll probably think twice about using that phrase

makes her happy and that's kind of one of the main things she can really talk about. I'll think . . . well, it's just what she wants to talk about and it makes her happy. Sometimes that's what makes me embarrassed.

The best part about being Stephanie's twin is having the opportunity to understand that Stephanie really doesn't have a mean or cruel thought. You know how people have negative thoughts and they think a little maliciously sometimes, or they think badly about people? She doesn't do that. It's really great to live with someone who's like that.

We went around to all of the different priests in the area and begged and pleaded and . . . some were really excited but didn't have the facilities for it. Finally Reverend Wade Abbott, from a local Baptist church, said, "You know what? We'll do it."

He proposed the idea to his trustees; some of them were happy about it and some of them said no, this is a lot of work, we don't want it. They said: We don't have hungry people in Sussex, and we don't want to bring them to our church because they're all criminals, and they're going to steal stuff, and they're going to break things, and we don't want to be part of it.

So now it was time for the students to get more involved. We started meeting with the trustees. We started explaining to them. It was kind of interesting because it was the younger students talking to the oldest members of our community and trying to convince them that we were right in the sense that these people aren't criminals. They kept saying, Oh, you're bringing them into our neighborhood. And we said, they're in your neighborhood already. This is where most of them live.

Well, after months and months of trying to convince them, they voted on whether or not to allow the soup kitchen and finally it passed. That was a very exciting day. We were all there when they voted on it. Then all of a sudden, we read an editorial in the paper that said, "We don't have a problem with hunger. I wish these kids would stay out of the way. They don't understand what hunger is." They just went on and on and on. And we felt so attacked. Now it was becoming political. Now there was opposition. So we had to go to a zoning board meeting where all the townspeople rallied and had posters and signs that said "Get Out of Our Town," stuff like that. We had our own lawyer there who did this all for free and he stood up there and pleaded our case and we individually went up—it was a long night. Eventually the town board decided to let us in.

But it was a very narrow margin. So we knew, going in, that there were a lot of people who didn't want us there. And that was hard. That was the end of 1999, the end of our sophomore year. We had our food, we were starting to get our money. Now we had to get employees, and get the health permits. We had to renovate the church. We got people to do it for free. It took months and months and months.

On February 14, 2000, we finally opened. But we didn't open the doors; we passed out bag lunches outside. That way we could get around the health permit until we could finally get everything up-to-code. We served bag lunches to about forty people a day. Most of the adults used the lunches as dinner for their kids. That helped them a lot. October 30, 2000, we opened officially. Two of us who had stayed with it the whole way through hung the "Open" sign. It was a very emotional day.

like a stroke when you're a baby. It makes me sad because I think, What if it was me? A lot of people don't understand. They just haven't ever been around a person who's disabled. A lot of people feel sorry for someone with disabilities. That's really not how you should feel. If you're going to talk to a person who's developmentally delayed, just treat them like a normal person. Don't talk down to them, that kind of thing. Don't be conde-

because it's just so offensive. It just shows a kind of ignorance.

Sometimes Stephanie, she gets real exuberant when she meets new people. She might come out and start telling them she loves music and she has so many CDs and she knows the number and the name of every album. And I'll think, you know, Stephanie, they don't need to know that, so just don't tell them about it. But then I see it's what

'Oh, that's so retarded.' That just completely sets me off."—Amy, 14

scending. If someone talks to Stephanie conde-scendingly, she knows it. She's got intuition that says, I'm smarter than that.

A lot of people use the phrase, "Oh, that's so retarded." That just completely sets me off. I know they say that because they don't understand. They think people like that are stupid. Completely not the case.

I'll explain to people that my sister is disabled and they'll say, "Oh, she's retarded." And I say, "Well, if you want to think of it like that, I guess you can, but I don't really like to use that term." If you ever meet someone who is disabled, you'll probably think twice about using that phrase

makes her happy and that's kind of one of the main things she can really talk about. I'll think . . . well, it's just what she wants to talk about and it makes her happy. Sometimes that's what makes me embarrassed.

The best part about being Stephanie's twin is having the opportunity to understand that Stephanie really doesn't have a mean or cruel thought. You know how people have negative thoughts and they think a little maliciously some-times, or they think badly about people? She doesn't do that. It's really great to live with some-one who's like that.

people did anything to help. It wasn't until after Harvest House that I really understood the concept of poverty.

Harvest House is the soup kitchen that I started with some of my fellow ninth-grade students. We decided that we would do a research project on hunger. We had no idea what would happen with it. We got a couple of hundred dollars' grant money and we decided to see what hunger is in the county where we live. We wanted to see if there really was a problem.

We researched hunger by interviewing people, going to the other soup kitchens in the southern part of the county, finding out where the hungry were coming from, and we made all these graphs and charts.

After a year of research we found that most of the poor in our county were from the town right next to ours and they desperately needed food. They couldn't get to the other soup kitchen because they couldn't afford the transportation.

I was always one of those children that wanted to help the poor. You know, save the world. I'd see those commercials where you send twenty cents a day to an organization. I always wanted to do that. I didn't really understand poverty; I just thought it was something that wasn't getting better because not enough

We decided to hold a one-day soup kitchen and see what would happen when we invited all these people. We did that on Make a Difference Day, October 1998, and we were overwhelmed. We had about a hundred people come from the county, saying that they all needed a soup kitchen in the northern part of the county. We polled them and asked, How many of you would come if we started a soup kitchen here? We were shocked.

Everybody wanted to come to the soup kitchen. We sat down one day with our school advisor and said we wanted to make a soup kitchen. She thought we were crazy, but she said, okay, okay.

We were sophomores at this point thinking it would be easy to set up a soup kitchen. It was so much work. You don't realize how much work it is until you get into it. We started polling all the soup kitchens from the state and asking them how they got started. We got a pretty good consensus of different ways we could go.

We started immediately.

Make a Difference Day sponsors a national contest. We submitted an essay about what we had done and sent it to the national committee. Then they picked winners—ten from the entire nation. Well, hundreds and hundreds of people are part of this; we didn't think we'd ever win. I was sitting in our classroom one day and we were working on the transportation issue, how we were going to get people up to the northern part of the county. We got a call. Our advisor almost fainted. Then she told us: "We won national!" We had won a $10,000 grant, from Paul Newman's foundation. Two of our students and our advisor and our principal went down to Washington, D.C., and they received our check for $10,000.

It was amazing what happened from there. Now we had $10,000. You can do a lot with that. We started getting so much money from the community, so much food. We didn't have a place yet, so we were storing it in the basements of all

"If you see something that needs to be changed, do it."—Erin, 17

the kids' homes because we didn't know where to put the food. Now the big dilemma was, where were we going to put the soup kitchen? I mean, who wants a soup kitchen in the basement of their church? It's a big hassle.

We went around to all of the different priests in the area and begged and pleaded and . . . some were really excited but didn't have the facilities for it. Finally Reverend Wade Abbott, from a local Baptist church, said, "You know what? We'll do it."

He proposed the idea to his trustees; some of them were happy about it and some of them said no, this is a lot of work, we don't want it. They said: We don't have hungry people in Sussex, and we don't want to bring them to our church because they're all criminals, and they're going to steal stuff, and they're going to break things, and we don't want to be part of it.

So now it was time for the students to get more involved. We started meeting with the trustees. We started explaining to them. It was kind of interesting because it was the younger students talking to the oldest members of our community and trying to convince them that we were right in the sense that these people aren't criminals. They kept saying, Oh, you're bringing them into our neighborhood. And we said, they're in your neighborhood already. This is where most of them live.

Well, after months and months of trying to convince them, they voted on whether or not to allow the soup kitchen and finally it passed. That was a very exciting day. We were all there when they voted on it. Then all of a sudden, we read an editorial in the paper that said, "We don't have a problem with hunger. I wish these kids would stay out of the way. They don't understand what hunger is." They just went on and on and on. And we felt so attacked. Now it was becoming political. Now there was opposition. So we had to go to a zoning board meeting where all the townspeople rallied and had posters and signs that said "Get Out of Our Town," stuff like that. We had our own lawyer there who did this all for free and he stood up there and pleaded our case and we individually went up—it was a long night. Eventually the town board decided to let us in.

But it was a very narrow margin. So we knew, going in, that there were a lot of people who didn't want us there. And that was hard. That was the end of 1999, the end of our sophomore year. We had our food, we were starting to get our money. Now we had to get employees, and get the health permits. We had to renovate the church. We got people to do it for free. It took months and months and months.

On February 14, 2000, we finally opened. But we didn't open the doors; we passed out bag lunches outside. That way we could get around the health permit until we could finally get everything up-to-code. We served bag lunches to about forty people a day. Most of the adults used the lunches as dinner for their kids. That helped them a lot. October 30, 2000, we opened officially. Two of us who had stayed with it the whole way through hung the "Open" sign. It was a very emotional day.

Every time I pass the church, I see the Harvest House sign outside and it's a reminder that I worked so hard for that and it's finally there.

A lot of people think that poor people don't work. You're poor, you don't want to work. You'd rather just sit at home and get freebies. That's not what it is at all. Most people that are poor have two, three jobs. It's just all minimum wage or below minimum wage jobs and they're not making enough money to support their families. Another interesting fact we learned is that the average American is two paychecks away from poverty. So if you lost your job and didn't get two paychecks, you could be just like them. A lot of Americans deny that. But it's true.

If you see something out there that is a problem, don't sit there and wait for an adult to do it, because kids can do it. You don't need to wait. You can start at any level. If you see something that needs to be changed, do it. Don't wait. I think that's the biggest thing we got out of it. If we had sat there and said, well, I hope somebody makes a soup kitchen, there still would not be one. Nobody would have taken the initiative. So take the initiative and get it done.

I've learned a lot from the experience. It made me grow as a person to think that I was part of something this big. I mean, if I can do something like that now, I can think of even bigger, better ideas. Do even more. That's what I hope to accomplish in my life.

I came home from a Valentine's dance last year and I was really swollen, my ankles and my stomach and everything, because of water retention. My dad was curious like, what is that? My mom took me to the doctors, and from there the tests and everything started. I was admitted to the hospital and a couple of days later they found out that I needed a liver transplant. They told my family and it was a shock, but they handled it well; they said that God was going to heal me and everything was going to go well. I had to have a liver transplant because I had a disease called auto-immune hepatitis—the kidney cells fight and then they attack each other. My liver was getting smaller and smaller.

On April 15th I needed my spleen removed because it had an abscess in it; it was really huge and it could have burst. They caught it in time because I was really getting bad abdominal pain. They took me to Children's Hospital in Seattle and they took the spleen out. I had to heal from that before they could put me back on the transplant list again. So then May 15th, that's when they said that they had a liver for me.

Around five o'clock in the morning the nurse came in to give me some pain medicine because I was hurting. I had a nose tube so they could feed me through the tube. Another nurse walked in and woke up my mom and said that we had a liver. We were so happy we didn't know what to do. If we could have, we would have been jumping up and down on the bed and everything. They pushed off my feed, and then they just prepped me from there. We called our family and told them we had a liver. My family came and at five o'clock that evening they took me into surgery. It took eight hours.

They wouldn't give us any information about the liver at first. They just said that someone had died on Mother's Day. But they didn't give any other information. A few days later the donor family wrote to me and asked if they could meet me. So I wrote them back and I thanked them for the decision they made. The first time we met them we went to a restaurant. They had told us to look for a little girl with strawberry blond hair. So we were looking and this family walked in. I knew it was them, but I wasn't quite sure because the woman had two roses in her hand. I didn't want to go right up to them, so as they walked in, my mom asked if they were the family and they were. Then they said, "Are you . . . are you Antonette?" I told them I was; then we

"Diana was 14 at the time she died. And I was 14 at the time I had my liver transplant."
—Antonette, 15

started giving each other hugs and everything, and the mother gave me the roses. She said, "This is a rose for you and one for my daughter Diana."

Diana was fourteen at the time she died. And I was fourteen at the time I had my liver transplant. Diana's family said they are going to try to come to my baseball games and watch me play. We're going to meet them again.

Ever since I was little, my parents called me "the star." Now they call me "the lawyer," because that's what I want to be. Right now I'm in the sixth grade and reading is my favorite subject. I've always loved to read, especially the big words. We have a reading place in our house, a place that is silent and quiet just for reading. Sometimes my mom reads to me, stories with big words.

I'd like to be a lawyer and help people read the cases that they're fighting for. To become a lawyer, you have to have good grades and pass all the credits. My mother told me to stay involved in my books and that's what I've been doing. When I'm a lawyer, I'll dream of having a big house and cars and everything. I don't know about children yet.

"Think big."—Briana, 11

Right now I'm a Girl Scout at a school in Mississippi where every girl in the school is a Girl Scout too.

Think big, be yourself; don't let anybody else tell you anything different. Just be yourself.

The things that I love to do, I'm able to do through Girl Scouting. I'd probably be biking and caving if there wasn't Girl Scouts, but with that you're able to share your commonality with the same sex and just to be able to be more open.

Last summer I participated in a bike tour. It was called Bike South 2000. It was to celebrate the year 2000. It was a 2,000-mile bike ride across six states: Florida, Alabama, Georgia, South Carolina, North Carolina, and back to Virginia. We had people from all over—Scotland, Australia, and from all over the country. There were people of all different ages, from seventy-year-olds to fifteen-year-olds. There was a little boy who was twelve who was riding with his father. I was the youngest female, and the youngest person to ride without any parent with me the whole time.

It was really a good moment when we crossed the finish line in Charlottesville, but it was also really sad because we had met all of these people. When you're with someone for five weeks, biking with them every single day, it's really sad to see it end.

"I wanted to prove that I'm just as good as anybody."—Jessica, 15

By riding in Bike South 2000, I wanted to show people that young females can bike as well as anyone. People think that Boy Scouts would be the ones doing something like this. I get a lot of my Boy Scout friends who say, "You can't do these big backpacking trips." When I told them that I was doing this bike trip, they didn't even believe me. At first, I just wanted to do it because I enjoy biking. But that changed when I realized how many people think that you can't do something because of your sex. I wanted to prove that I'm just as good as anybody, any male, and that I can bike 2,000 miles just as well as anybody else.

Even all of my girl-friends said, "Why would you want to do that? We don't do that type of thing." I just want people to realize that they *can* do it, even if it's difficult. It's possible to achieve these things. You just have to be optimistic and not think that things are impossible, because they are possible. Where there's a will, there's a way.

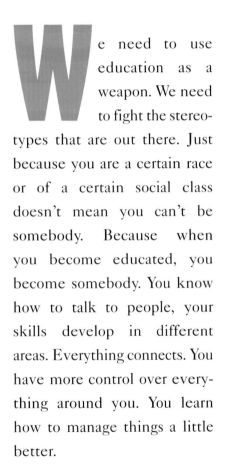

We need to use education as a weapon. We need to fight the stereotypes that are out there. Just because you are a certain race or of a certain social class doesn't mean you can't be somebody. Because when you become educated, you become somebody. You know how to talk to people, your skills develop in different areas. Everything connects. You have more control over everything around you. You learn how to manage things a little better.

"When you become educated, you become somebody."—Roannelyn, 16

It doesn't really matter what kind of school you go to. You are who you are and some schools have a lot of money and some schools don't have much. What does matter is what kind of people you are surrounded by, because that influences your character, what kind of person you will become. I like to be with older people because you can see things from a lot of different perspectives. They speak from experience, which is even better, because wisdom comes from experience.

oetry. Oh, man, poetry. It's a way to vent anger; it's a way to express love. When you write poetry, you're sending a message out to everyone. Other people can agree with you or disagree with you, but it doesn't matter. Poetry helps me get my feelings out. The truth is in the poetry.

What bothers me in the world is prejudice. I think being prejudiced against anything is just stupid and wrong. The way I see things is that you're human. It doesn't matter the color of your skin.

You're gay, you're straight, it doesn't matter. If you bring a child into the world and you teach them not to like a person because of the color of their skin, the child grows up and feels this hate toward those people for no reason. The main point is, we all have the same type of blood. It's just a way of saying, you know, this is a rich culture, learn from me, and we can teach each other. If we're here, we're here on earth and we have to get along. If we try to get along more, maybe the world will be a little bit easier to deal with. I can't always change people's minds. The only way I can do that is through writing. Writing is where my heart is. Songwriting. I especially love hip-hop. It's the type of music you can't really describe. When I hear some song, it's like my skin starts tingling and I'm dancing and I feel great. Hip-hop reaches out to certain people. A lot of people say that hip-hop is a bad way for people to express themselves. In actuality, if you listen to the person's album, they have songs that talk about going back to their hood and changing it. They will say how they would make it better. They might have a song dedicated to their mother. And they would have another song about partying. Some songs shouldn't be taken seriously and other songs should. Not everyone is killing each other in rap. A lot more is going on. If you're human, anything is going to happen. Anything can happen.

"Writing is where my heart is."—Tamika, 15

As part of a job-shadowing experience at my Montessori School, I started volunteering at an arts center. I wanted to work with little kids and I like painting. I went through the parent-child training program and now I work with children that are three to five years old. It's great to see their creative minds growing. They're just thinking of new things they can do every week. Also, instead of watching TV or doing something that's not really productive, they're in a classroom being creative, doing fun things, and learning.

There's a Montessori place called Blackwood Farm twenty minutes from where I live. We planted a lot of trees there. They're all

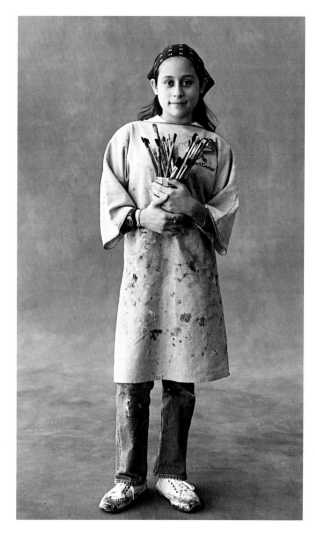

"I think that by doing all these things I'm trying to help the world be a better place."
—Erica, 13

different ages because if they were all one age they would all die at the same time. We've also helped out at a Montessori camp in the area. There we paint picnic tables, buildings, stables, fences, and more than one hundred beds.

I think that by doing all these things I'm trying to help the world be a better place. People don't care enough about the world. I don't think they really realize what they're doing, so I'm trying to do things that will help them realize. What concerns me most is pollution. I think that people should recycle. That's one of our projects at school right now. I think that people should do that because it's helping out the rain forest. If we cut all the trees down, then we won't have any oxygen to breathe.

I think you should just go out and if you see something wrong, like if you see trash, you should pick it up. If you see something that's run down, you should go try to make that place look better and do whatever you can to try to make that place more presentable.

A few years ago I ruptured a disc and we took a lot of X rays. Through all the different doctor appointments, I found out that I have bone abnormalities. They had to shave part of the backbone out so that I had room for my nerve. At first I couldn't even walk. I was very disappointed back then because, you know, at my age you make all these plans that you want to happen. But I just kept thinking, fifteen years from now, twenty years from now, this won't seem like such a big deal. It's just going to be a part of my life.

Before my surgery everything was a big deal. If you didn't have a date for Friday night, that was a big deal. Missing a ball game was a big deal. And I don't know, it's just—it made me put things back into perspective—things with my family and everything else.

"The choices you make today completely affect you two years from now, twenty-two years from now."—Natalie, 16

Monticello's a friendly town. You feel comfortable when you walk down Main Street, even though it's very old. It's historic-looking. You feel at home even if you've never been here before. But even here, drugs are part of life. I think it's because there's not very much to do. In the big cities you can go to movies, skating rinks, go eat at different restaurants. Not here. You can go hunting. Or, you know, there's the Big Lots parking lot. I mean, there aren't really that many choices. But the choices you make today completely affect you two years from now, ten years from now, twenty-two years from now.

Last year, I entered the Miss Monticello scholarship pageant. You are judged on interview and sportswear, evening wear, and you also have a platform that you're going to support for the year of service. My platform was Girl Scouting. I've had a program for our troop every month so far. And that's been really amazing.

"If everyone helps each other instead of hurting, I think it could really make a difference." —Amy, 13

I've been studying dance basically all my life. I'm studying modern dance and also ballet because there you learn how to *really* dance. I think that every song has emotion for someone—maybe you're scared, or you're happy, or you're afraid. The song makes you feel what the composer might have felt.

My dance teacher puts us in large groups to come up with dances to perform at our spring concert. Our teacher likes a lot of different styles, so we're doing a little bit of modern, a little bit of Spanish, and a little bit of Irish. Sometimes all these kinds of dances can help bring everybody together. There's something that everybody can relate to: the Irish, the Chinese, the Indian, the Spanish. There is a mix of cultures that helps people relate, which is something we need to do.

Sometimes, even though we may try to hide it, people feel the same as others. We don't want people to know our problems, so we hide them away and take them out on each other. Some people have strong feelings, but they hide them because they don't want anybody to know *what* they're feeling. Things like that eat you up and can make people commit suicide or hurt people, like in school shootings. If people fight, or if they are sad and take it out on everybody around them, then other people get bitter and the anger spreads around.

I think that helping the people around you helps change this. For example, I'm part of a youth organization called FYI (Fresh Youth Initiative). We have a food bank and we make deliveries to seniors who can't leave their houses. They don't give us anything but a thank-you, but it makes me feel satisfied. I know that I'm going to be old someday and maybe I'll need somebody watching over me in the same way. If everyone helps each other instead of hurting, I think it could really make a difference.

When we were little we were forced to go to church. You know, "Come on, you've got to wake up, you've got to go to church." But now that I'm older, I go to church because if I don't go, I'm not going to feel right for the rest of the week.

Two years ago my mom and I were thinking about what I should do for the Gold Award project at my school. My religious education teacher was a judge and she suggested a clothes drive for battered women. There are abused women who go into courts to try to get restraining orders and they feel embarrassed about themselves, the way they look. We started to have meetings with lawyers, police officers, everybody, everybody under the sun. It was incredible. And then we started the drive.

The mission was to get clothes, to find a place to put the clothes, and to get the clothes to the women. I went to shelters. I went to women's organizations. I put up flyers in the police department. It was scary when the women would tell me stories about what happened. It was scary that somebody could be that cruel to somebody else. Those women got beaten almost daily and they actually survived. That was inspiring. They actually had the will to keep going.

When I went to organizations to speak about my project, women would come up to me and tell me their stories and they would thank me for everything I was doing.

I couldn't imagine myself getting beaten every day and staying with the man out of love for him. I don't know. I just don't see it; it makes me upset, too, that their self-esteem is that low that they can't move on.

"The mission was to get clothes, and to get the clothes to the women."
—Katherine, 17

ife is not a dress rehearsal. I got that from a coffee cup we have at our house. I don't really pay attention to that stuff, but one day I was looking at the cup and I said to myself, That's really true. You only have one time. You should be careful what you do and try to do the best because you're not going to get a chance to do it again.

I think we should just reach out to people. I try to talk to people in my school, even if I don't know them. You just have to say, "How are you doing? What's going on at school or work?" Just something like that. Sometimes when I have a bad day and someone stops and asks if I'm okay, I might not talk about exactly what's wrong with me, but it's just nice to know that someone took that few seconds to notice that maybe I was upset or not having a good day. Even if I don't tell them, it's okay, because someone cared. You can make a difference, one person at a time. You don't have to do it on a large scale. If everyone started with just those people around them, or in their communities, or in their homes, or in their families, you would see what a difference it makes. You would be surprised. I think it would make a world of difference.

"I think we should just reach out to people."—Lauren, 17

"I realize that I should get more into my culture and who I really am."
—Julie, 15

I was adopted from Pusan, South Korea, when I was three months old.

My family lived in New England when I was little. We moved down to Georgia when I was about five. Living down here is totally different from living in New England. When we were close to New York, there were many other children who were adopted like me, and there were lots of other Asian people. Where I live now there aren't as many Asian people and there aren't that many people who are adopted.

In middle school it gets really cliquey. I felt like I didn't really fit in because I didn't look like everybody else. I guess, though, that everybody always has a thought in the back of their minds that they don't fit in. Everybody wants to fit in, even though they would deny it. They all want to get in with the "in" crowd. Now I realize that I should get more into my culture and who I really am.

I was looking at the people that were in the "in" crowd and I had nothing in common with them. I know I'm different, but it didn't really bother me that much. It doesn't really bother me that much now. But I never talk about it with my parents.

I went to a Jesuit high school and now I go to a Jesuit college. I'm not a hard-core religious person, but I think that learning to help people and being aware globally of what's going on in all countries is a good thing. My mom and dad have always told me to be aware because I'm half Mexican American and half German. I think just being of a mixed ethnic background makes you more aware of and more sensitive to issues.

A lot of times I'll be with a group of friends who wouldn't necessarily know I was Mexican. They'd make a racist remark and then they'd realize and apologize. It makes me more active in going out and trying to raise awareness and help other people.

Sometimes you just joke around and you say things. But sometimes people say things consciously. The thing is, they feel guilty and they feel bad. I think for the most part people are generally pretty good, but raising awareness is still important. I made a video where I interviewed girls about their racial background, also people with disabilities, handicapped people. You should keep an open mind and an open heart. I think that's the key thing to tell people.

Right now I'm trying to raise awareness about sweatshops. I've been passing out flyers in front of Nike Town—it was just information on what was going on in Mexico at the time, how people were trying to unionize and Nike wasn't letting them. Maybe if you're walking by, take that flyer. Don't just walk by. We're trying to work on problems too. Just be aware and maybe take the flyer and read about it. Some people say you can't do anything about problems. Everyone's got their own opinion. But I think you can.

"We're trying different things, different ways of reaching out."—Audrey, 18

"My friends don't really understand what this is like."—Anna, 14

My mother died of breast cancer not long ago. She was sick for a long time. She got it three times. The first time they did chemo. Then the second time they tried radiation and she had to have some surgery done. The last time, I can't remember, I think she was getting chemo. She was at home the whole time that she was sick, which was hard because we couldn't go anywhere or do anything. Other than that, it was all right because it meant that we didn't have to go to the hospital everyday. One day she said, "When I'm gone, you know, don't worry about me. I'll be in Heaven with my mom and everybody." It really freaked me out because I think she just knew what was coming.

My friends don't really understand what this is like, so they kind of expect me to be my old self. But since I don't really have a ride to go places sometimes, or the money . . . well, they just don't understand. I pretty much like to keep to myself. I mean, I don't want people feeling sorry for me. I can't get around to places as well and can't go out and do things because my dad doesn't like shopping or any of that. I always ask my friends if I can go with them, but they always say no, because it's a family outing.

Shopping was something my mom liked doing a lot. We went nearly every week. Once in a while when my brother and sister and dad would go stay at the cabin, we'd stay home and she'd say, "We're going to get up early tomorrow and go shopping." So then we'd do that and then the night before, we would go to a movie and eat popcorn. That was a lot of fun. I mean, we still rent movies, but they're not like Mom movies.

It's hard now. Sometimes I wish everybody would come out of their cocoon and knock on mine and say, "How are you today?"

"I want to get rid of the hate that everybody has."—Olivia, 12

My mom's a hippie, and my dad hates hippies. My parents got divorced. All my life I've known my mom is a hippie because she loves candles and she makes her room colorful and burns incense. She dresses like a hippie and she's very into peace. Me, I'm the same way. I love all that stuff. You have to love people and you have to love animals and you have to love your neighbor. Of course sometimes you can't love somebody all the time.

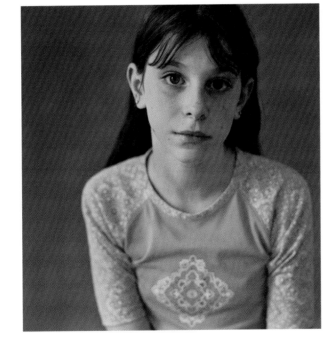

I have a lot of friends that think this is all very weird. But I usually don't hang out with people who like to make fun of other people, the way they dress or if they have a lot of money or no money, because I think that those kind of people are very mean. I don't like to hang out with mean people. I like people that like you for what you are inside.

I want to get rid of the hate that everybody has. I know that a lot of people are trying to do that, but I really want people to understand that you don't have to hate anybody, because everybody's the same inside. A lot of people don't know that.

My mom showed me this picture of a little girl in China who had died. She was just three weeks old and she was in the middle of the road. There were pictures of these people just passing by and nobody even cared. What I really want to do is to find a way to help people whose parents don't want them. I know that's an orphanage, but a lot of orphanages are very crowded. I want to open up an orphanage or a shelter for people in China like that little girl. They really want boys there, so I want to help the girls.

I think that it's wrong that people get left out and are not even given a chance.

y father had a rough family, very poor. So he said, I'll come to America and start a new business. He came to New York first, and then to Florida. He couldn't speak any English. He was twenty. My mother came when she was twenty-five or so, just to come and visit. She stopped at a Japanese restaurant and decided to work for a little bit. She got to know my father, they got married, and then I was born.

My home was full of Japanese culture. My mom cooked Japanese food all the time. We spoke Japanese all the time. I didn't speak English until I was maybe four or five years old.

Everything was perfectly normal until two years ago. My father started having really heavy headaches. He went to the doctor and that night my mom called me and said there was a tumor in his brain. I thought, "Oh no, what's going to happen to him? Is he going to die?" I wasn't prepared for that.

He went into the city a couple of days later and then we found out that he had to have surgery in his brain. After twelve hours of surgery he came out and he had this little white cloth on his head; it looked really painful. And all he could say was "Who are you guys? What's my name?"

They didn't get it all. They only got about sixty percent of the tumor. They said they couldn't take it out: If they did, it would damage him. They tried radiation, and chemotherapy, and another surgical procedure where they put a tube in his head to relieve the fluid in his brain. He had a really rough time. He would say, "What is for dinner?" Five minutes later, he'd say, "What's for dinner?" Then he'd be watching TV again and he'd say, "What's for dinner?" He just repeated himself like that all the time. And my mom would say, Well, you have to understand he's not like you guys.

My father was probably forty-nine or fifty and he just looked really old. After that, he went downhill. The doctor said they couldn't do anything anymore, so he had to go into the hospice. Two weeks later he died.

After he died, my mom always talked about him. And I'm like, why are you talking about him? She said, he really would appreciate it if you talked about the positive things. Now, when I talk about my father, I talk about the positive things; it's good.

My mom and my sister and brother moved back to Japan so that Mom could take care of her parents, and I decided to stay here and finish my senior year in high school. I live with a family here. At first I was just confused because when I went to my friend's house, it was so different. My mom said, I know it's rough, but you can't come back because you only have a fourth-grade level of their school work so you wouldn't be able to keep up. I thought: I need to stay strong for my family and then I'll go back to Japan for college. I'm not sure though, because I still haven't been accepted to the colleges in Japan.

I really want to use Japanese and English together. I want to get to know the Japanese language better. I want to understand the culture and how to write; I really want to know how people are in Japan and how it feels to live there. So if I do get to go to colleges there, I want to study a lot in Japanese, maybe French a little bit, because I'm taking French right now. Maybe become an interpreter or something international.

"Now, when I talk about my father, I talk about the positive things; it's good."—Hitomi, 18

> "If some boys were acting rude to me, now I'd be able to walk straight by them and say to myself that I could defend myself."—Amanda, 13

I study karate from Monday through Thursday. My mother works at the center where I take lessons. I've learned to have discipline because the teacher tells you what to do, how to treat other people. I've learned to have respect for teachers and others. We've learned how to defend ourselves, how to defend each other. It's like gaining power, because now I can defend myself from whoever is attacking me.

If some boys were acting rude to me, now I'd be able to walk straight by them and say to myself that I could defend myself. I don't need to put myself at their level by responding to them. The things they say don't matter anymore.

I have a teacher for social studies and English. He teaches us that there are people who don't have the same opportunities we have. We have education. He teaches us that we have to respect people. My mother also teaches me that we should help people who don't have money, because they need help.

I would like to help. If I had a lot of money, I would like to have a place where poor people could go and sleep. I would give them money to buy their food and help them get a job and help them pay their rent. If they don't have a mother or a father, I'd put them in a big house and then people who have money could take them in and they could live with them. I'd like to do that.

These are scrubs. Everything from the booties to the little hair cover and the lab coat. Ever since I was about four years old, when I actually knew what a doctor was, I knew that I wanted to be one. At first I wanted to cure people and go out and save the world, especially children. Then a couple of years ago I realized that there's not really anybody to help the adolescents. You go from seeing a pediatrician to seeing an adult doctor, and there's no in-between area. I've come up with the idea of being a pediatrician with a focus on adolescent health.

When I was in eighth grade, I had to have reconstructive surgery on my chin and I hit it off with the woman who did it, Dr. Caroline. She said, why don't you come on rounds with me? I would get out of school around 12:00 and go from 12:00 to 5:00. All the nurses would say, "Hi, Ashley! How are you doing?" I would pick up my clipboard and go to an office visit with the doctor. I would sit down and before she came in, I'd say . . . "Hi, my name's Ashley and I'm going on rounds with the doctor. Can I help you out?" I'd take down notes about what their problem was. Then when she'd arrive, I would brief her: "Okay, she got her ear pierced by her best friend. Got a problem here." The doctor would just go in and say, "Okay, let's take care of this." It worked out; I loved it.

While I was growing up, I had a mother who I could talk to about some things. But even when you have one of those mothers that seems to know everything, you still want a neutral source. I had a brother who thought he was too cool for me sometimes. Other times he wanted me to be there. So I couldn't really go to him either. And dads are great, but they don't know as much about females, just like we don't know about guys.

So that's what I would really like to be; that neutral point where people in their teens can go—you know, kind of an open-door policy. For whatever they need. They don't have to necessarily make an appointment. I'd like to be there.

"I'd like to focus on adolescents."—Ashley, 17

"I worked with the children."
—Jessica, 17

I started thinking about abuse last January when I went to a leadership conference with a bunch of other high school girls and we had to do community service. I picked the Center for Prevention and Abuse because I'd be working with children. I went there and I fell in love with the whole entire idea of helping children who came from abused families. I loved helping them—it was hard but we needed to get the job done.

The center is a safe haven for abused women and their families. The women are in charge of taking care of making dinner once a week, and they have to do their own laundry, and they have to find a job while they're in the center. They have a sup-

port group for kids too, which deals with everything from sexual abuse to verbal abuse. That's where I worked, with the children.

You can't believe that people would hurt children or their wives and it's horrible but it happens.

I feel ashamed of our society that this still goes on and I get mad sometimes, but most of the time I just feel utter disgrace for those men who beat their wives and their children. You shouldn't do that. I grew up in such a loving home. I'm so appreciated, and that would never happen in my family.

It kills you when you see a woman that you know has gone through the program and she's going to go back to her husband. The ratio is only one to four that a woman who leaves will leave for good. Most of the time, the women come back.

I'm drawing a mural on the side of one of the walls in the center. Its message is to try to learn to forgive. And to remember that it's not your fault. The mural says, "Hope Comes in Many Different Forms." Then it's got pictures of all different kinds of people. In the center of the mural is a picture of the center; it is a pink house they call the "Pink House in the Woods." We're going to have all the kids put their handprints up there.

I volunteer in the hospital, helping the elderly and the kids, and pushing the cheer cart, which is like a mobile gift shop. My mother is a receptionist at the hospital. It's good to know that she's going out and trying to help people and that helps me to learn that I need to go out and try to help people also. Since I needed five hours of just go away. But if they say, "Hey, how are you," then I go in and start talking to them. If you want someone to feel good about themselves and you want to feel good about yourself, you should go talk to other people and make them feel good.

I only need 20 hours of volunteering to graduate, but I've done 260 hours over two years.

"If you talk to them, it's like all the pain goes away."—Frenché, 16

community service each year in order to graduate from high school, about two years ago my mom suggested that I volunteer at the hospital during the summer. I've been working there ever since.

The kids love for you to talk to them while they're sick. They look up to you as a role model. And the elderly, they just want someone to talk to because they're lonely. Going around with the cheer cart is sad sometimes, but you try to do your best to cheer people up so they can get their mind off what just happened. It's like, they know they're in pain, but if you talk to them, it's like all the pain goes away. I just like to see people happy and help people out, so I like to go talk to them. I go by and say hello, and if the person doesn't want to be bothered, I

"I was so lucky to have the opportunity to see what it's really like somewhere else."
—Aly, 18

've always had this dream to travel around the world. I want to go to as many places as I can. Before I went to Africa, I hadn't really gone anywhere. My best friend has family who lives in Africa. They're missionaries. As a graduation present my mom and my best friend's mom decided that we could go to Africa before we went off to college. I had no idea what to expect . . . I had no idea what I was going to see. It was definitely a shock when I got there. It was just so different. Everything about it was different.

We stayed with a missionary family, so we got to do some of the things they do on a daily basis, which is just so unbelievable because they devote all of their time to helping other people. One of the first things that we did was help at a baby clinic. Women from miles and miles away walked in the heat with their babies on their backs to get them shots and checkups. Hundreds and hundreds of women came with sick babies, crying babies, dirty babies. We were able to hold the babies and bring them to get their shots.

The whole time I was there I just wanted to help more. I was so lucky that I was even able to have the opportunity to see what it's really like somewhere else.

Doing things for other people—that's the main thing. It's a dream to get a lot of money one day. Right? To be in a job where you're happy and make money. But to just have it, and yet know that there are people with nothing, wouldn't be right for me. Now I would love to be able to do something for other people.

My name is Diana, also known as Princess Defeat.

Hip-hop is basically going against the grain. It's nothing standard. It's doing the unexpected. It's like going on a roller-coaster ride with the rises and the changes because evolution means it's never the same. It's not like country or pop where, you know, you hear the same formats of music. In hip-hop you can have a fast-speed or a slow-speed rap or gangsta rap or rap about love or struggles. There are different dramas to it. There's no code or pass-word telling you how to be hip-hop. I know I'm hip-hop. How can you be hip-hop? You've just got to do you. Whatever is best for you is you.

It started out in the Bronx: kids rhyming over bebop and stuff like that. Now it's so glamorized: You see rappers driving around in all these expensive cars, in regular commercials, and things like that.

The way I'm dressed; okay, this is an example of going against the grain. This shirt says PNB, post no bills. It means basically, post no advertisement about yourself, no misconceptions about yourself. Don't do what you don't want to do. The regular person might wear pants and a shirt, but on a hot day like this, I might pull up this way, pull it this way, fold it over, walk around the street looking

"To me, hip-hop is cathartic."—Diana, 16

like this because I'm hip-hop. We just do whatever is us; that's what I'm going to do. That's what hip-hop is.

I want people to understand hip-hop because it gives them more of a perspective on where we're coming from. I mean, to me, hip-hop is cathartic. I don't feel like it's anger. It's just an expression. That's all. Instead of being destructive to ourselves and people around us, we're writing about it. It's therapeutic. It's not just about anger; it may be anger they're releasing when they're writing it, but it's just releasing; it's cleansing.

Last year I was a page for the day in the Senate at our state capitol. I also went to the Girl Scouts Legislative Day at the capitol, and met a lot of senators and representatives. One day in history class it just clicked: I want to be a senator and I want to move to Washington, D.C., and lead the people— I think I'd love to do that.

I'm really big on education. All through elementary school and even in preschool my teachers always encouraged me to speak out and I was always the one trying to lead the class when we were split up in the groups. I like to have my voice count.

At church I'm in the youth group. Most of the people there are in high school and I'm in junior high school. I'm always trying to speak up for the junior high kids because there are only two or three of us.

One thing that's always bothered me is how people don't ever listen to kids who are in high school, junior high, elementary school, because they think that they don't know anything. But really some of them know a lot more than the adults. I want people to understand that they can listen to the kids and understand them and take what they say seriously.

We aren't just a whole bunch of punk rockers who don't listen to anybody. We're real people just like anybody else.

Once you get everyone together and once you get them to talk together then they'll begin to see each other's views and they'll come to a middle ground.

"I'm really big on education."—Megan, 13

I started doing community service when I was in third grade. My friend told me it was fun. So I went because I wanted to help out. I didn't have anything to do after school. I just wanted to help and meet new people and make new friends and have a different experience.

I help out at the soup kitchens in my neighborhood. I get to hear people talk about their lives. When I clean the table, they talk and I tell them my name. The homeless, they're not different. The only thing is, they don't have a home. They're normal people. They just weren't as lucky as we are. Something happened in their lives, or maybe they did something wrong . . . I really don't think about it because sometimes it's sad seeing them.

Working with homeless people has taught me to appreciate everything that God gave me, and that you have to appreciate everything: your life, your family, everyone. Just try to help other people who are less fortunate than you. Try to find an organization that does positive things.

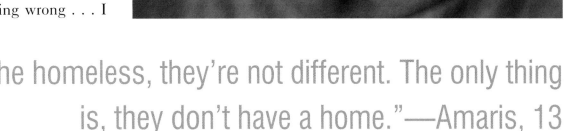

"The homeless, they're not different. The only thing is, they don't have a home."—Amaris, 13

"I think that the youth of my generation seem to have huge power."
—Wilson, 16

I think that being a woman is inherently political in the same way that being black is inherently political. You don't necessarily have to be all about raising your fist, but as a woman you need to struggle and you will struggle. Saying we've come so far, we've done this, is only relevant if that's what you feel within yourself and if you've come far in yourself. If you've really become whole in your womanhood and feel empowered by the incredibleness of being a woman.

I know that I'm so, so lucky because my parents do incredible things that they're passionate about. I think that when you have parents who are doing what they love and pursuing what they feel is their gift, they're a lot more willing to let you do what you love and find out what makes you tick. They help you find your passion because they've had to find it in themselves.

I think that the youth of my generation seem to have huge power. I take a poetry class at an organization called Youth Speaks and it's an intense community of people. I think it's such an incredible thing: to give youth a voice. We have more of a voice and we have more ways of channeling our passions. That's amazing because twenty-five years ago we might not have been able to write our emotion into poems, or express ourselves through painting, or in the activist work that we do.

Kids my age need to stand up for other people. If we hear someone name-calling or using a racial slur, we should say something. A lot of people just think, oh, it's not a big deal, what's being said—it's just a joke or whatever. But I think that everyone needs to take it a lot more seriously than they do. Some people just let it slide and then the name-callers just do it more, and then it gets back to the person who's being called names. That person feels horrible, first of all. Then he or she can take that feeling and turn it into anger and then turn it into violence.

"Everyone can help and just do little things."—Christine, 16

Everyone can help and just do little things. I sometimes ask, "Why did you say that about that person?" Saying something like that will make a person think, "Why did I say that about that person?" A lot of times, there'll be no answer. "So you just said it for no reason?" I'll say. And they'll say, "I guess so." And then they feel stupid and they probably won't do it again.

My parents are really open-minded and I think that's made me more open-minded. Growing up in my elementary school, I was one of fourteen white kids in my entire school. I've been friends with a lot of different people from different backgrounds and different social classes. I'm not saying that I can understand everything that everyone is going through, but I can understand it more because of the people that I interact with.

I've worked hard. I don't believe being valedictorian shows that you are extra smart or a genius. I think that it's just that you worked hard during the year and you deserve it. I don't think I'm a genius, and I don't think I'm anything out of this world. I'm just a regular student who does the work and stays focused. I like school and I like studying. That's why I became valedictorian. It's just a title.

I came from the Dominican Republic and my parents didn't have the opportunities that I have. It's my choice to be whatever I want to be. And I've chosen to be a pediatrician when I grow up; I want to study and I want to learn.

The teenage mind-set of being part of the crowd, that's most . . . challenging. I decided that I'm unique. I don't have to be like everybody else. If people are going to parties, doing drugs, alcohol, it's not me. Most people don't have the strength to stand up to others and just say . . . I'm myself. I don't have to drink, I don't have to smoke, don't have to be like everyone else.

I believe that teenagers should always try to be themselves and not follow others. Be a leader. And keep focused and study; it will definitely take you somewhere.

"I decided that I'm unique."—Maribelis, 16

"It's important to understand that everyone has different opinions. If we didn't, we would just all be the same."—a Girl Scout troop in California

Now it's so much harder for her to walk than it is for us. It hurts me a lot to see how much pain there is for her.

It's really difficult caring for her. I've always been an independent person, so I was fine staying by

"I've come this far and

myself when my parents went to the hospital and stuff. I've grown up with her being sick, but Dad was a different story.

The summer before last, we drove out to Colorado. We were going to be out there two weeks. He started getting really bad headaches, but the doctor in the ER said they were just migraines. On the way back from visiting Mt. Rushmore, he was just getting worse and worse. Eventually we decided to drive straight home because he was getting to the point where he needed to get back. He was almost in a daze; his eyes were all glazed over like he wasn't really there.

The day after we got back, he went to his regular doctor. I remember being at golf practice—I was on the twenty-third hole—when someone ran out to get me off the course. I knew something was

I was two years old when my mom had her first surgery on her hip. She had benign tumors, and they were right on her sciatic nerve, which is the nerve that controls your legs. Since then she has had seven surgeries on the same place on her hip. Then one time, the tumor they pulled out was malignant and they decided to amputate her leg because after they got that tumor out, her leg would have just been dead weight.

wrong because my mom would never have done that otherwise. She'd just wait till I got home. I had this sinking feeling as I drove home, and when I got there, there were cars everywhere and a whole bunch of people at my house. My grandmother gave me a hug. Everybody was crying. My dad was lying on the couch just sleeping. Then my mom

I can take anything that comes my way."—Erin, 17

told me they were going to take Dad in for emergency brain surgery right away. It really didn't hit me then.

My little brother and I just sat there for a while and then people went to the hospital. I didn't go. I couldn't handle seeing my dad sick. He had always been the one to take care of Mom, and I didn't think I could see him in a hospital bed. He was in the hospital for three weeks, but I didn't go to visit him. I made excuses—it's the beginning of the school year, it's the middle of golf season—but I think I just knew that I wouldn't be able to see him like that.

We take life a little bit more slowly now. Our whole family does. People take the smaller things for granted, but we've learned that those are sometimes better. When you look at the small things, you find random acts of kindness. You just have to deal with life; take your obstacles as they come. Everybody faces different obstacles.

People don't understand the value of a good attitude or a smile. Sometimes it's hard to see the good. Like, with all the sicknesses in my family, sometimes it was hard to see what good would come of it. But there are always repercussions that are good. A few of my parents' friends put together a benefit for my mom and dad at a local hall. They had food and entertainment and a big silent auction. There were so many people in the building. It was shoulder to shoulder and you couldn't even move.

Our family stood on the stage and sang the song "Angels Among Us." It was really powerful because everybody watched us sing and then started to sing along. It was a great outpouring of love. I took a picture of the line to get in and that's what blew me away. There were so many people there. They were all waiting outside and it was March, so it was kind of chilly out. But they were all waiting just to come in and see us and to say hi and show their support.

People think this is all a big thing, but for us, it's just life. It's just the way we live. You know, cancer is a part of life. If they find a cure for it, that's good. But if not, you just live with it and gain strength from every obstacle that you look in the face, and say, I've come this far and I can take anything that comes my way.

I was born this way. I was born without my right forearm. I haven't used a prosthesis since I was really little because I learned how to do everything this way; eat, tie my shoes, . . . carry stuff. I can do headstands with a little difficulty. One thing I can't do is the monkey bars. I always wanted to be able to do the monkey bars, but some things you can't do.

I went to physical therapy when I was little to learn how to do things because my parents wanted me to grow up normal and just to do as much as I could possibly do. They let me use any kind of prosthesis that I wanted to try; just to try everything out, see which I liked the best. After I was eight years old, I decided it wasn't really worth it to wear a prosthesis at all because I couldn't play sports in it; I couldn't swim, couldn't do anything with my prosthesis on. It just made things harder. I know how to do everything with one hand.

If I have to use a word to describe myself I guess I use "disabled" because that's just the best fit. But when I think of myself, I don't think of myself as

"By the time I was 11, I held three American records and one world record in disabled swimming."—Kim, 13

disabled or handicapped or anything. And my friends don't either. Once people get to know me, they realize what I can do. I don't let being disabled stand in the way of anything; or I try not to.

I've loved soccer ever since I was four years old. I've met some of my best friends from soccer. And I just love the competition; I love all the hard work that goes into it, even though practices can sometimes be tiring. I love the tournaments, I love games, I love winning. I just always loved soccer.

My parents wanted me to swim to build up the muscles in my right side since I do everything with my left hand. I liked it, so I stayed with it. I started swimming when I was nine or ten. By the time I was eleven, I held three American records and one world record in disabled swimming. I started out just for the exercise, but I like the thrill of swimming through the water fast. So I stuck with it and it's taken me pretty much all around the world.

I was a page for my state's general assembly this year. That's one of the best experiences I've ever had. I had so much fun serving the delegates and their aides. I learned a lot about the legislative process. I would like to go into law and maybe politics. But I have also wanted to be a psychologist because I like helping people and making them feel good about themselves.

Usually when I meet someone and after we've talked for a little while, I tell them I was born this way and that I don't let it stand in my way. That's the way I am. If the person's going to be a good friend, she won't let it bother her at all. I used to tell a lot of jokes. I'd say I fell into a pit of sharks and they bit my forearm off, or I got attacked by an alligator or something like that. Jokes always help because laughing makes things more comfortable, and it made people more comfortable with it. So I just make up funny little stories.

My parents have always believed in me from the beginning, and they opened new possibilities for me and let me try new things and really supported me, whatever decision I wanted to make. So that, I think, has helped a lot.

"As the people in the group get together and do more activities, we start growing and branching out."—Lorena, 13

Based on my grades and behavior, I was selected to be part of an organization called Roots and Shoots, an institution started by Dr. Jane Goodall. It's called Roots and Shoots because as a tree grows it has roots that will start at the bottom. Like trees, as the people in the group get together and do more activities, we start growing and branching out. We help the community, animals, and the environment. There are millions of members around the world with at least one group in every country. The group really shows us something that we can do for our community. I've gained trust with my community and I'm really satisfied with what I've done so far. Coming from where I come from, not many kids think about their future. This program has helped me look ahead. It's pretty interesting because you get chances and opportunities.

I've also gotten a lot of inspiration from Derek Jeter who plays shortstop for the New York Yankees. I consider him my role model. He wrote a book and I learned that every person has a chance to become what they want, especially girls. I want to be a sports reporter. There are not many women as sports reporters right now, but through his book I've learned that I can be what I want.

I know there are children out there who need help, so I wanted to get involved as a mentor. Now I do one-on-one work with a little girl, Britney. There are a lot of children who aren't as lucky as I. It means a lot to me to make a difference to a little child.

The first day I met Britney, she was just a ball of fire. We did her math homework. I showed her a new way of solving problems—it meant so much to her. She couldn't believe that somebody was giving her the attention. No matter how bad things get, she can find a way to look at the positive side of things.

"There are a lot of children who aren't as lucky as I."—Hilary, 14

She has a really bad home life. She doesn't get the attention she needs and she's being traded off by her mother and father, who both have new boyfriends and girlfriends.

I've picked her up from her home a few times. She wanted me to see her bedroom and things. I guess when I walked in her room I was expecting a little girl's room. But it's not like that. It's just a room and there's not much to it. It's dark and it's not the best-kept house. She has some toys and she has a few things on the wall, but not much.

I'd really like my family to meet Britney because she means so much to me. I know it might be hard for her to be in a home where everything's, you know, good and happy and nice. But I think she knows that there are homes like that.

I was already certain that I was going to be a teacher when I started with Britney, but I've actually asked myself if I'd rather work with younger children or maybe special education, or help children that are troubled in some way, because I know they need the most attention of all.

It's really rewarding being with Britney, but it's also really emotional sometimes, too. It's tough to say good-bye, but I'm making a difference in someone's life and that means a lot.

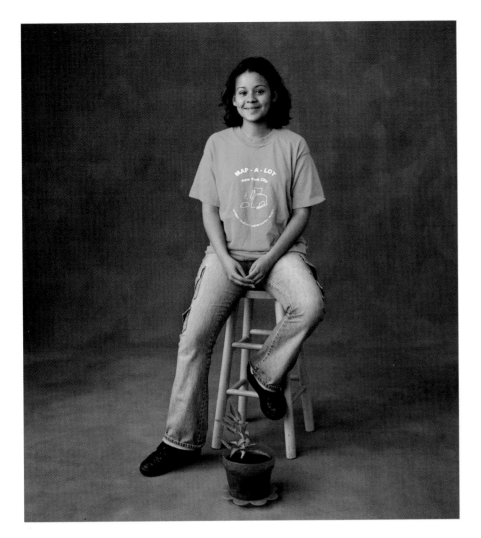

"Gardens are a way to get out of the streets."—Erica, 16

play on the field, or go in the greenhouse and water the plants. Working in these gardens has made me realize how useful they are and that we need to have more of them around. Gardens are a way to get out of the streets, especially if you know the people who are involved in the garden. It lets you get comfortable and meet new people who you can help out.

I really like helping people and making the community a better place, so I want to be a social worker or a psychiatrist. I read a book called *A Child Called It* by David Pelzer. The book was about a boy named David whose mother and father called him "It" instead of by his name. They used to abuse him and they used to make him do things that he didn't want to do. Eventually he couldn't take it any more and he had to tell somebody. He got out of the situation by going to a foster home . . . and then another and another, and then he just grew up and went to college.

The book made me think more about the kids who have been in abusive families. It just made me want to help them.

When I was in the eighth grade I got involved in the school garden and a community garden. I like the planting and just being around everything green. When you walk by a garden in the city, you see a lot of trees and fruits, but then you walk down the block and there are only buildings. There's only that one garden on that whole block. But inside the garden you could walk in every direction and enjoy it. There's a pond you can sit beside, or you can

I graduated valedictorian from my high school and now I'm at a women's college. My high school was predominantly African American; probably about 70 percent or so. That was basically the story of my high school. A lot of people from the community that I lived in didn't want to send their kids to public school because they didn't want them to be in a school where the other students didn't have the same socioeconomic background.

It was one of those places with little community support. Most people sent their kids to private schools because the local public education wasn't "good enough" and would lead their kids nowhere.

No one ever paid attention to what we did. We had the number-one newspaper in the state four years in a row, but somehow no one ever knew. We were always state champions, but no one ever paid attention.

I think that anywhere you go, you can either make things happen or you can just sit there. People have a lot of misconceptions. They think that the public-school students can't do as well as white, rich, private-school kids. But I know so many people from my class and the classes before that went to Ivy League schools or got recruited for different sports. I think it really just depends on the people, not the school that they go to. I think that people should take more time to think about the public schools and what you can do to fix them, because students that go to public schools

"People have a lot of misconceptions." —Dana, 18

shouldn't have to try so hard to compete with private schools. It's a battle, but it shouldn't be.

I go to a special high school for leadership and public service in my city. I'm doing very well in school: I'm ranked number four. Once I get out of high school, I know I'll go to college.

I think that education is the best thing that you can get in your life. I'm going to be the first person in my family to go to college. My parents did not have the opportunities that I have here. My father just reached fourth grade and my mother reached the sixth grade in the Dominican Republic and they only speak Spanish. They both have to work. They brought me here and I'm going to take all the opportunities I can so that I can be an example for my siblings. Then my parents will know that their sacrifice paid off.

The director of the organization PENCIL (Public Education Needs Civic Involvement in Learning) called my principal looking for one student to represent all of the city's schools. The principal was like . . . oh, I have the person. She talked to me, and I went to a seminar to discuss the way we view education. I made a speech about my teachers and what they have done for me.

Teachers are very special in my life. They are often the only support system for students. When parents aren't there to help, the teachers are there. I'm lucky to have so many teachers around me that I can talk to, not just about academics but also about emotions. Since my parents don't speak English, I go to my teachers and they help me with any situation I have. My teachers have really made me believe in who I am. The principal is a role model too. She has taught me that one day I will succeed as much as she has.

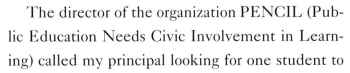

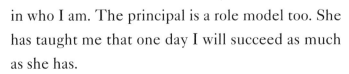

"My parents will know that their sacrifice paid off."—Esterlina, 18

When I was twelve years old, the hearing in my left ear was starting to get kind of plugged and the inner ear canal was starting to get itchy. I thought maybe I had like an ear infection or something like that. So I went to my doctor and he gave me some antibiotics. They weren't working so I went back and he sent me to an ENT specialist. I could kind of see something starting to form in my ear. Like, if I looked in the mirror and looked into my ear canal I could see that there was something dark in there. The specialist biopsied it and sent the results to a specialist in San Francisco.

This all happened in about a week; it was kind of scary. We didn't really know what was going on. Cancer was the last thing that we expected. We went down to San Francisco to talk to this specialist; he's one of only four in the world who specialize in the type of cancer I had in my ear, so he was able to diagnose it right away.

I think I was diagnosed on a Wednesday, and then I came back to San Francisco on Friday to start my treatment. So it happened really fast; within like a week or two. The doctor said I had a cancer of the soft tissue. My cancer started growing around my left carotid artery and then it just kind of fingered toward my ear canal. It was pressing against the lining of my brain, but it wasn't to the point where it was doing any damage. If I had let it go longer, then it would

have. We're really lucky in that we caught it first. As it was, it destroyed the hearing in my left ear canal.

So I'm deaf in my left ear now, but, you know, that's why God gave us two ears, right?

I started off with radiation and chemotherapy. That was horrible because I had three chemotherapy drugs at once. Those are three of the most horrible drugs that they can give you. They attack the new growing cells in your body and that's what cancer cells are; they are rapidly dividing cells. Unfortunately, that's what hair cells are too and so that's

"I'm a cancer survivor." —Heather, 18

why chemotherapy usually kills off your hair follicles. So I had to have treatment while I was doing the radiation as well. I would go in three-week cycles on the chemotherapy. One week I would be in San Francisco getting chemo for five days. Then the next week I would be at home and my blood counts would drop down, the white blood cells. So I would have no resistance to germs and stuff so I would be anemic and I would usually have to go to our local hospital just so that I could be isolated and be getting IV fluids and nutrients that way. I would usually have to have a blood transfusion at that time to bring up my platelets. And then the next week I would usually try to go to school and catch up on schoolwork and stuff like that and lead as much of a normal life as I could. Then I would go back down to San Francisco.

I was sick all the time. I would have to leave school sometimes just because I got too ill. I felt so horrible. I was in bed all the time and my muscles started to atrophy so I had to have physical therapy. When you're feeling flu-like, you don't want to move around. I had to try and keep going. I had so many people who I didn't even know support me and help me. Some of the people that we know got together and they had a dinner auction and they made thousands of dollars just to help us pay for gas money, hotel bills for my parents, and food for when my mom would come down to San Francisco with me. There's a local store in town that had Heather Day and all the sales from that day were donated to me. It helped me so much. It was like I had to survive, and it wasn't going to be just for me. It was going to be because I didn't want to let anyone down. It was kind of like fighting for the whole town. I really like that about small communities. I had so many people help in different ways.

I was diagnosed in May and then I ended chemotherapy the end of April the following year. So it was almost a full year of chemotherapy treatments. For a while I still had medical issues that I had to really be careful about. They say that for every day of chemo that you have, it takes two days to recover. So after a year of chemo, it took two years for me to start feeling normal and good again

and build up some of the muscles that I had lost during chemotherapy. Just trying to get back into the swing of a normal life, not having to worry about whether or not my IV was still in the proper drip system and things like that.

I think it gave me a lot of perspective. When I look back, whenever I have any kind of a problem, whenever I'm feeling sorry for myself, I'm able to look back and think of all the friends I met in the hospital. They had it so much worse than I did. I got off so easy. It may have been a year of hell, but in the big picture, I'm okay now. I'm not going to have any lasting problems. There are kids who are paralyzed from cancers that they had in their spine, or who are going to be blind forever and things like that. I met kids who didn't survive. So, I have it pretty easy.

It actually has helped a lot of my friends. Someone came up to me just the other day and said, You know what? I was feeling really depressed because I was feeling bad and life has been kind of crummy lately and then I came across this newspaper article of when you were first diagnosed and it helped me remember . . . what's going on right now is just stupid and worthless. It helped her. And that, for me, that was really great because to help me find perspective is one thing, but when my experiences can help other people, that's when I know that having cancer was not this curse that was put on me. I didn't do something wrong. It was a blessing, really. Someone told me that when I was first diagnosed, and I thought they were crazy to think that having cancer could be anything good. But as I'm looking back, it really was a positive experience on the whole. It helps to realize that I have a lot of support and that if I ever have problems, I have people that I can turn to, and that people can trust me with their problems. I can't put into words how it's helped me in life.

I was twelve at the time. I decided I wasn't going to let it get to me too much because it's so easy to get depressed when you're on chemo. So to keep things light, I got a face-painting kit and I would have pictures painted on my bald head. For Valentine's Day I had hearts and Cupid. I had a shamrock for St. Paddy's Day and I had a big spider in a spider web for Halloween. So it just helped. I think it helped my friends, too, because I was going around school with these paintings on my head. It was funny. It helped them realize that it was okay to be bald and talk about it. Some people I know had a hard time. They thought I would be really edgy and not want to talk about having cancer at all. But I think it helped people to realize that it's okay and helped them not be afraid of what was going on.

I'm a member of FFA, which stands for Future Farmers of America. Whenever I was in the hospital, my mom would always bring me fresh flowers from the florist downstairs. It was great because it was a way to keep things sunny and bright and make it more like home where there are flowers everywhere instead of looking out the window at a wall from the next building. It helped me stay cheerful and remember that I had people back home still thinking of me. So whenever I see flowers now, it's a reminder that there are really beautiful things out there still. I love making things grow. I don't know if that's just a reflex from being in the hospital all the time or not having anything to do or what. But I love working with plants because they cheer people up. When you give someone a plant, you're giving them this living thing that they can take care of, and I like to be able to make people be happy wherever they are. To make someone's day just a little bit brighter, that's pretty cool. So I'm a future horticulturalist. I would eventually like to own my own plant nursery so that I could sell plants and maybe have a floral shop on the side.

I've always been afraid of heights. When I would look up, I would get dizzy and scared and I would get butterflies in my stomach. I went to North Carolina with Outward Bound and there was a five-hundred-foot-high rock that we had to climb. At first I couldn't do it. Then after some time passed, I thought, no, I have to do this. I climbed all the way to the top. When I looked down, I couldn't believe it.

That trip was part of a six-week literacy program in North Carolina that I got to attend in ninth grade along with eleven other students. It was a program to help students stay in school. It was a class, but not like regular school. We got to go on trips, but we also did a lot of writing. Most of the time the trips help you to face your fears and overcome obstacles.

The philosophy is that overcoming obstacles and fears makes you stronger and builds up character so you can overcome other things that seem bigger than they really are. During the six weeks we spent in North Carolina, we wrote essays about experiences we had and how we felt about the things we faced in our trips. The main thing I learned was not to let things that seem really big bring me down. If I just continue on and don't let anybody stop me from what I want to do, then I can do anything I set my mind on.

If I could fix something in the world, it would be the poor quality of education we get in inner-city schools. We don't have enough money to pay for books or materials that we need. The amount of money that we get is not enough to buy one book per student. Most times we need to use old, worn-out books that are missing pages and are written on. People expect us to get high grades and pass our SATs with 1500s, but we don't have what we need to prepare ourselves to get those types of scores. So, in one of my classes, we're writing letters to our representatives to see if they'll give a donation to help our school.

I think people should always try to find somebody who will be supportive of them. Even if you don't have family, there's always a friend out there who will "take your back"—someone who will support you and be there for you when you need her.

"The main thing
I learned was
not to let things
that seem
really big bring
me down."
—Valerie, 17

"Nobody's a failure. I think if you don't quit, then you will achieve your goal someday."—Michelle, 12

I am part of the Fresh Youth Initiative—FYI.

We do community service in my neighborhood. We paint murals and we paint mailboxes. I don't like graffiti because it makes the neighborhood look bad. We paint over graffiti.

We paint murals: designs with flowers, designs that have buildings and cars.

It feels good because I'm making a difference. It would be much worse if I wasn't there. It makes the community better. It helps it a lot.

The Fresh Youth Initiative took me to the University of Michigan with a group of kids. We learned that you have to pay for the books, the dorm rooms, and the college education. It's a lot of money for one year; a lot of money.

When I go to college, I don't want my parents to pay for it. I want to have a basketball scholarship. You have to have good grades to get a scholarship; I'm second honors in my class. My parents have to afford my brother, my little sister, and me. So that's a lot of money. I want them to not pay for me.

My parents are always supporting me. They've always been there at my basketball games. They teach me never to give up. Let's say a girl is trying out for a team and she didn't make it and she gives up . . . she won't try any more, then she thinks she's a failure. But nobody's a failure. I think if you don't quit, then you will achieve your goal someday.

Every year at my school, we have a senior citizen's prom. The members of student government dress up and get a DJ who plays music from our grandparents' generation. The guys from student government dance with the women, and the girls dance with the men. We have food for them and it's all a lot of fun.

I'm the person that wanders around and goes to all the tables because I love to dance. I dance all the time. I try to set the old men up with the old women and get them out there to dance because I can't possibly dance with everyone. I try and pair all the people from student government with the other people. I remember one guy in particular that I danced with: He was this old man and he had a cane and he was really not wanting to dance. But we went out there and he did the hokey pokey. It was really fun.

People treat seniors as though they're not the same, just like people treat teenagers like they're not the same. If someone's not your age, you look at them as different from you. But they're just people in different stages of their lives.

I think that music brings people back to when they were younger. Music really brings back memories for older people as well.

Everything I do connects to music. I'm thinking about going into music therapy because it's such an interesting field. Music is definitely healing. They use a lot of music therapy with war veterans and kids that can't talk. Instead of doing physical therapy, they teach them how to play a musical instrument or a rhythm drum. There's a lot of healing in music because it's a way for people to communicate if they can't communicate like everyone else.

"Everything I do connects to music." —Saara, 16

I want to be a newscaster.

Every day of my life I watch the news. I watch *The Early Show*. I wake up, get dressed for school, have breakfast, and watch the news for about a half hour. I've been doing that since I was in the second grade. My dad watches it with me.

I don't like the lack of knowledge that some people have about things going on in the world. They don't read the newspaper, they don't watch the news, they don't have knowledge about cancers or things that could harm them.

In social studies they're talking about things that go on in the news: the presidential election, the Oklahoma City bombing, school shootings, terrorist attacks. You should know things that are going on in the world. You shouldn't be oblivious to what's going on.

I like telling people things. I like to talk a lot. I like to show people what's going on. So maybe if I become a Katie Couric, that would be great. Seems like a fun job too.

I think it would be exhilarating to know what's going on in the world, to have intelligent conversations with people instead of normal "Hey, what's up?" conversations. What bothers me is when newscasters report a story about some horrible thing that happened and then they just say, "Okay, let's go to the weather."

I think they should talk about it on the news, comment on it before they go on to the traffic and weather. Put it into a bigger context.

I also think once in a while they should have something positive on the news, things that people should know about that could help them— good things about art and music, and things people do for each other. There's got to be *something* positive as well as all the negative things that are going on.

"You should know things that are going on in the world. You shouldn't be oblivious to what's going on."

—Tori, 13

My parents were divorced when I was four. I live with my mom and my sister, so I never really grew up with my dad. I think that divorce is mostly an issue between parents. A lot of children blame themselves for a parents divorce, but I still feel it's the parents' issue and not the children's. I know that I never blamed myself, but I think all children react differently. Personally, I think I've become stronger.

Also, I think that friendship is really important, as well as families. I think at an adolescent age children rely more on their friends than their families because their friends are willing to agree with them. Parents are usually telling them what to do or not to do. But friends are willing to agree with them because they're at the same age and they understand what the other is going through.

I know I'll always have my friends, even if they leave for college. I know that when it's a serious issue I can trust them not to tell other people. Being able to talk with one of my friends and just tell her something that I need to say is so stress relieving. With schoolwork, with sports, with everything that's going on, people can be so stressed. Just being able to tell my friend a problem that's been bugging me is so much easier because I don't need to worry about it anymore, because I know that they can help me through it.

I think people who don't have friends are maybe not willing to reach out. When you have friends, you're willing to reach out and give of yourself. I think some of the people who don't have friends are scared. When people trust each other, it creates a bond. It's hard to make people who don't have friends realize that friendship would come if they could open themselves up to other people.

"When people trust each other, it creates a bond."—Pam, 14

"We like to help. We are Girl Scouts." —Marines, 17, and Valerie, 16

MARINES: I've been in the Girl Scouts for ten years and we wanted to earn our gold medals. It's something that every Girl Scout wants. We decided to look for a place that needs help. I wanted something to do that really helps the community. Something that makes us feel good.

VALERIE: When the principal first told me about this program that helps people and encourages them to be independent, I decided I wanted to help. Now we spend a lot of our free time fixing up this building, making it a home.

MARINES: This is an institution for children that were abused. They live here. Normally they are ages six to eighteen. After that they're supposed to go, but a lot of times they don't.

These young people don't have a house; they don't have parents. I think that by being here I'm doing something right. I always feel good when I walk in here. Sometimes people say that girls can only do certain things. We have been in the Girl Scouts for twelve years and ten years and we're here because we like to help people. We have a good time, but we don't just sell some cookies and that's it. We do things that really help the community. We like to help.

Every girl has a voice, and it should be heard and also considered. I think that when every girl says something it's because she feels it and it should be heard. For years women's voices haven't been heard, maybe because for a long time they weren't considered an important part of society. Now that we are seen as what we really are, we can talk and insist on being heard.

"I can be equal."—Iris, 16

Being a woman in this world isn't easy; that's why we need someone or something that helps us in the difficult situations of our life. I became a Girl Scout when I was nine years old. As a Girl Scout, I started going to camps and on trips to some places I've never seen before and I learned a lot about them. In our group meetings we talk about almost anything, like nutrition, self-esteem, health, fitness, other countries . . . anything. At the age of ten, I could say that Girl Scouts helped me to understand the changes I was experiencing, physically and mentally. Then, in the next years it gave me a lot of opportunities that any girl who's part of the Girl Scouts has. The Girl Scouts organization is like a school that is focused on a girl's life, doubts, changes, and challenges. It helps girls understand all of that, using life experiences as examples. The program is always focused on girls' necessities.

I feel equal. I have success in different aspects of life, like in school and Girl Scouts. I can be equal. Now, as a girl in this society, I can be equal to anyone.

"People don't need to fight over how they pray . . . just as long as they pray."
—Angel, 13

I was told that I was chosen by the spirits to carry the pipe for my people to begin the Sundance. I live in the Lakota Indian reservation in South Dakota.

Sundancing is when you dance to ask for forgiveness, or to pray for someone else and suffer for them.

We dance around a tree, and when it begins, the men dig up the tree that we danced around last year and they place it down the hillside with the other old trees. Because it's sacred, it holds everything that people danced for. And then they choose another tree, a fresh tree. And they plant it in the same soil.

When they bring in the tree, I carry the pipe in front of it, carrying all the hopes and dreams and the prayers of the people.

The people who are watching support the people who are dancing. They sit there and we dance and go around this tree, because the tree is supposed to be the symbol of life. It's usually really hot. That's why it's called Sundancing. We don't get to drink that much water, but we do drink sage tea. We don't eat much—just a little bit just to keep us going. It's a special time, a time to fast. We have breaks every now and then. We don't go to sleep. We only have five or ten minutes and then we have to get up and go again. This lasts for four days. We dance each day—the whole day. You wake up when the sun rises, it's five-thirty or so. And you sleep when the sun goes down. After a couple of days, it's as though something that you carried on your shoulders just got taken off. And when you sleep, it's nice.

I dance to help me understand everything. I know some of the Lakota language, but not much. So I pray that I learn more Lakota, that I understand it. I want to change the fighting over religion, because it doesn't really matter, just as long as you pray to a god. People don't need to fight over how they pray . . . just as long as they pray.

Dear God, when I did something wrong, you forgave me.
When I was in the dark, you gave me light.
When I needed you, you were there.
When I was hurt, you healed me.
When I am sad, you cheer me up.
When I die, you will let me stand beside you.
Thank you, God.
Amen.

about Girl Scouts of the USA

This book, dedicated to every girl, everywhere, is the centerpiece of the 90th Anniversary of Girl Scouting, March 12, 2002. Such a milestone cannot be celebrated without including girls—all girls—and their dreams, concerns, and valuable potential as our leaders of tomorrow.

While Girl Scouts of the USA enjoys millions of current girl and adult members, with many millions more Girl Scout alumnae scattered throughout the world, this organization is dedicated to commemorating the vision of what every girl is and can be, whether or not she is a Girl Scout.

Girl Scouts is the world's preeminent organization dedicated solely to girls—all girls. In an accepting and nurturing environment, girls build character and skills for success in the real world. In partnership with committed adults, girls develop qualities that will serve them all their lives—like strong values, social conscience, and conviction about their own potential and self-worth.

In Girl Scouting, girls discover fun, friendship, and power of girls together. Through the many enriching experiences provided by Girl Scouts, girls grow courageous and strong.

For information about Girl Scouts call 1-800-478-7248 (1-800-GSUSA4U), or visit our Web site at www.girlscouts.org.